INTERNATIONAL HEAVY TRUCKS

of the 1960s

Ron Adams

Iconografix

Iconografix
PO Box 446
Hudson, Wisconsin 54016 USA

Library of Congress Control Number: 2005936378

ISBN-13: 978-1-58388-161-3
ISBN-10: 1-58388-161-1

06 07 08 09 10 11 6 5 4 3 2 1

Printed in China

Cover and book design by Dan Perry

Copyediting by Suzie Helberg

Cover photo-Connolly Transport Inc. of Los Angeles, California, operated this COF-4070-A Transtar pulling a Utility trailer. This tractor had the optional disc wheels, air conditioner, 83-inch sleeper cab, chrome bumper, and chrome dual stacks, which indicates that it most likely had an optional Detroit Diesel engine. Wheelbases ranged from 142 to 184 inches. This rig is hauling Hamm's premium beer. *Ron Adams collection*

DEDICATION

Behind every success there is someone responsible for making it happen. In the case of International there are many who could share the responsibility for success. You could credit the engineering and design department for their work in designing all the great trucks that International produced over the years. Then there were the workers who dedicated themselves to building a great truck through workmanship. Then there was the sales staff, which worked with the customers that got the business leading to constant production of the product. No one group can take credit for full success because it takes all three to work together to make it happen, and this they did. So we can credit all three groups for this success. However, had it not been for two men, this success would never have happened. The two men I speak of are Cyrus H. McCormick and William Deering. Had they not taken on their ventures in the mid-1800s, none of this would have been possible. They are the two men responsible for bringing International into its infancy and then into a successful giant. From the Highwheeler in 1907 to the big wheelers of today, so I dedicate this book to these two men, Cyrus H. McCormick and William Deering. May they be remembered forever.

INTRODUCTION

International brought a lot of the late 1950s models into the 1960s: the "S" series that started in 1955, the "B" series in 1959, the BC series in 1959, the VCO in 1956, the CO in 1955, the R series started in 1953, the AC "Sightliner" in 1957, the "F" series in 1959, the V series in 1956, the DCO in 1956, the RDF series started in 1953, and the Metro that started in 1938 with a little restyling over the years. They came in four classes: lightweight, medium, heavy, and Xtra heavy. Over the past decades, Internationals were found performing all kinds of jobs from small pickup truck work to big oil field and mining work. These things did not change in the 1960s. In fact, International offered more models in each series to make them more versatile. But as time went on, International had to keep up with the Jones' (other truck makers) in order to compete. The big RDF series was replaced in 1961 by the new D series. A whole line of new "stars" came on the scene in 1962. We start with the Loadstar in 1962 that stayed in the lineup into the 1970s. It replaced the former BC series. In 1963, the CO Loadstar baby cab over engine came into the lineup. It was intended for store-to-store delivery and pickup and city delivery work.

In 1963, International reached a milestone. The one-millionth truck rolled off the line at the Fort Wayne plant. It was a Fleetstar 2000—another star added to the lineup in 1963. The Fleetstar was to replace the more heavy duty BC series models. The M series for the construction industry was also introduced in 1963.

Through the early 1960s the "R" series, CO, VCO, and the DCO were all moving along well in sales. The DCO-400 series was the best and biggest selling highway tractor in the country. Nearly 33,000 had been produced. But production came to an end in 1965 when International came out with the all-new CO-4000 series cab over engine to replace the best selling Emeryville. The new CO-4000 followed the same cab styles as the other manufacturers. The 180 Payhauler that used the 12V-71N Detroit Diesel was also introduced in 1965. The R series that was produced for 12 years was discontinued in 1966. A new addition to the M series was the tri-axle, tri-drive. The old style Fleetstar 2000 was replaced by the new style Fleetstar "A" in 1967.

International had many "stars" in their lineup. Another star added to the lineup was the CO-4070-A Transtar in 1968. This replaced the CO-4000 model. Still another "star" in the lineup was the Transtar D-400 conventional. Both Transtars' appearances were similar to their predecessors. Another "star" added to the family was the TurboStar. The turbine did not seem to make much headway versus the diesel engine because the diesel engines at the same time were becoming lighter in weight and more fuel-efficient. While the turbine was losing ground, the R series and V series were discontinued in 1968. The M series was still making a big hit in the oil and construction industry. Yet another "star" added to the family was the all-new Unistar in 1969. This was a 4x4 all-wheel drive. The three engines available for the Unistar were the Cummins NTC-335, the 8V-71N, and the V-12 Detroit Diesel. A Jifflox dolly could be used as a tag axle 6x4.

As we leave the 1960s and head into the 1970s, we learn that International has purchased Pacific Truck and Trailer Manufacturing Ltd. of Vancouver, British Columbia, Canada. A new Transtar is introduced as the 4200 and 4300 series as an all-new design. Also, a new Cargostar CO is introduced. A new Paystar 5000 will come that will replace the "F" and "M" series.

The models and series mentioned so far are mainly the larger straight trucks, over-the-road trucks, and off-highway and oil field trucks. International also made pickup trucks: the Scout, the Travelall, the Travelette, school buses, rescue and fire apparatus, and even a motor home. Many different models in each series were also offered in the bigger series trucks. Internationals covered them all with you, the customer, with the "Dealer's Choice." All these series trucks and different models account for the over 1,677,000-vehicle production for the decade of the 1960s. A very impressive record!

Designing a new look and appearance for a series, and a model change, was not always the easiest task. To the engineers it might have looked good. But the design and appearance had to be viewed by the big executives of the company. If they liked it, it was accepted. If they did not like it, engineering was told so in short order. Such was the case in 1960. The engineers designed the X-300-CO and the X-300 Conventional using clay. They were made with lots of enthusiasm but when the president of I.H.C. took a look at them he said they were the worst looking trucks he had ever seen. The project was then terminated and it was back to the drawing boards.

The pictures you see in this book mainly cover the bigger straight trucks and over-the-road and off-highway trucks; the popular ones like the V series, R series, D-400, DCO-400, CO-4000, and the line of "stars," to mention a few. As you look at them, enjoy and admire them, as many are long gone.

As we begin the 1960s we see that the big RDF-405 is still being produced. Romney Produce had this one pulling a Utility reefer trailer. A second fuel tank was added along with a box sleeper on this super long wheelbase. It used the Cummins NHB-600 Diesel engine that put out 220 horsepower. *Brian Williams*

The BC was also carried over into the 1960s. Hennis Freight Lines Inc. of Winston-Salem, North Carolina, used this BC-180 in their city pick up and delivery fleet. This model had a 5,500-pound capacity front axle and a 16,000-pound capacity rear axle. This BC-180 most likely featured the V-345 V-8 engine. The names of the three gentlemen in this photo are unknown, but judging from the smiles on their faces, they seem to be happy with this BC-180. *International*

A relative to the BC series is the ACO series. This one has the 48-inch cab and the standard cast spoke wheels. The standard engine was the V-401. Cameron Transfer & Storage Co. of Minneapolis, Minnesota, owned this tractor and Great Dane trailer. *Ron Adams collection*

This F-230-D was working in the Chicago area for Palumbo Excavating Co. It was powered by a Cummins NH-220 diesel. The front axle was rated at 16,000 pounds with the rear tandem rated at 44,000 pounds. This tractor had a 175-inch wheelbase but was offered as high as 259 inches. Trailer capacity was 26 cubic yards. *International*

The popular Emeryvilles could be seen in all parts of the country. This DCOT-405, nicknamed "Red Devil," was doing its tour of duty for Transamerican Freight Lines Inc. of Detroit, Michigan, in the reefer division. The engines were Cummins diesels with the standard being an NH-180 and the optional NRTO-335. Cast spoke wheels were standard but here we see the optional disc wheels. This rig ran from Texas in the southwest, Nebraska in the west, to the East Coast in the Transamerican system. *Neil Sherff*

The V series also came along in the 1960s. This V-220 was set up to run on LPG with either the V-461 or the V-549 engine. Optional disc wheels were selected. Its job was to pull this milk tanker trailer for the Carnation Company. *Ron Adams collection*

Still another to come along in the 1960s was the R series. This R-190 was pulling a Trailmobile gasoline tanker trailer for Miller Transporters Ltd. of Jackson, Mississippi. Fender mounted mirrors and a sun visor add to the appearance of the tractor. The standard engine was the International Red Diamond RD-406. The front axle was a 7,000-pound capacity with the rear being an 18,500-pound capacity. Although the names of the five gentlemen are unknown, it is very easy to point out the driver. *Hutchings-Newman*

Robertson Tank Lines Inc. of Houston, Texas, owned this CO-190. It is seen here pulling a Butler 38-foot, 1-inch, 8,180-gallon, 3-compartment aluminum tank trailer. The standard engine was the International Red Diamond 372 putting out 165 horsepower. Robertson chose the optional disc wheels and also a sleeper cab. *Butler Steel Products*

Here we see a DCOF-405 owned by Holiday Farms of Ft. Stockton, Texas, pulling a Wilson grain trailer. Although it had a few bruises and scratches, it still stands tall and strong like the rest of the Emeryvilles. *Brian Williams*

This BCF-220-D is seen traveling through the Wisconsin countryside to its destination for Olson Transportation Co. of Green Bay, Wisconsin, pulling a Fruehauf converta-flat trailer. The NH-180 Cummins diesel was the standard engine. This one had the standard cast spoke wheels. *Lefebyre-luebke*

Here we have a rear shot of an R series, either the RT or RF. The standard cast spoke wheels were chosen for this one. It's pulling a Progress Model S-26 tank trailer used to handle hot fats, grease, and oils. The capacity is 5,000 gallons. The owner is Faber Industries Inc. of Peoria, Illinois. The tractor has a wheelbase of 146 inches. *Progress Industries*

Valley Steel Products Co. of Missouri had a fleet of trucks that consisted of owners/operators hauling steel products. A wide variety of different makes made up the fleet. One of the trucks in the fleet was this BC model. The driver decided on the optional sleeper cab. The truck was nicknamed "Tennessee Stud." *Neil Sherff*

This nighttime shot shows an ACO-205 taken near Ypsilanti, Michigan. For driver comfort, they chose the 72-inch sleeper cab. This one was working for Ringle Truck Lines Inc. of Fowler, Indiana. *Neil Sherff*

The year 1961 was the last for the RDF series. Meade Baldwin of Millersville, Maryland, owns this 1961 RDF-402. Although it's a restoration piece, this photograph lets you see what the real super-sized tractor looked like. At this time, International was starting to offer Detroit Diesels as an option to Cummins diesels. *Ron Adams collection*

As we said good-bye to the RDF series we now say hello to the all-new D-400 series Emeryville, which replaced the RDF series. The D-400 had a fiberglass tilt hood that was followed by the same cab used on the Emeryville cab over engine series. The standard engine was the Cummins NH-180 but because of the broader and wider hood, a variety of bigger and more powerful engines were available up to 355 horsepower. A sleeper cab was also available. This DF-402 is owned by Lee Hutchens of Redding, California, and used as a log carrier. The loader is an International 250. *International*

Tractor number 2012 was built to do a job for California Motor Express Inc. of Oakland, California. Its job was to pull a set of double trailers (in this case they were Trailmobiles) and stay within the legal length. To stay within the legal length they had to be fitted with a short enough wheelbase and wear a 54-inch cab. The engine in this tractor is unknown, but the standard was the Cummins NH-180 diesel with options of up to 335 horsepower. This company chose the optional disc wheels. *Ron Adams collection*

Little Audrey's Transportation Co. of Fremont, Nebraska, was a refrigerated carrier that hauled from the Midwest to the West Coast. Their fleet consisted of various makes of tractors. In this case it was a DCO-405 that pulled a Trailmobile reefer trailer. It was powered by a Cummins diesel that was covered with an 80-inch sleeper cab. The owner chose the optional disc wheels. *Neil Sherff*

The R series ran strong into the 1960s. This R-200 was doing heavy steel hauling for the steel division of Yellow Transit Freight Lines Inc. of Indianapolis, Indiana. The standard engine was a Red Diamond 406, but because of the tandem axle to carry more weight it probably had the optional RD-450 or RD-501 gas engine. It featured standard cast spoke wheels. This driver chose the optional box sleeper. *Neil Sherff*

This V-220 was owned by the Standard Oil Co. of Indiana. It is shown here pulling a Butler 8,465-gallon capacity, 7-compartment aluminum tank trailer. The standard engine was the V-461, but again, because of the tandem axle for carrying more weight, it probably used the optional V-549. The cast spoke wheels were standard. *Butler Steel Products*

This photo offers a nice view of what the CO-200 looked like from the side. Ellsworth Freight Lines Inc. of Eagle Grove, Iowa, owns it and it is seen here pulling a Fruehauf reefer trailer. The standard engine was the Red Diamond 406. The 9,000-pound capacity front axle and the 22,000-pound capacity rear axle were standard. *Ron Adams collection*

The popular Emeryville DCO-405 was available in many configurations. This truck had a long wheelbase to accommodate the dromedary body. Notice how far back the Utility trailer is hooked. This kind of a setup was used for hauling lightweight freight. The cab featured a 72-inch sleeper. *Brian Williams*

Here we have a pair of BC-170s. The standard engine was the V-304 and each had a 7,500-pound capacity front axle with a 15,000-pound capacity rear axle. Andrews made both bodies with Thermo-King refrigeration units. Numbers 7 and 8 were owned by Union Packing Co. *Andrews Trailer Co.*

Here we have the R-190. The standard engine was the Red Diamond 406 with the optional engine being the RD-450 or the RD-501. A sleeper cab was also optional but in this case it featured the day cab. It is owned by Reely Van Lines of Missoula, Montana, and pulls an Alloy moving van trailer. Reely has been in business since 1903. *Commercial Photographers (Seattle)*

This V-190 is pictured doing oil field work. The standard engine was the V-401. There is a good possibility that this truck could have the big, powerful V-549. The company is unknown. *Elmer Weaver*

Moving the goods was the job of Lyon Moving & Storage Co. of Los Angeles, California. This DCO-405 hauled the goods in this matching set of Utility moving van trailers from the 1950s era. The tractor featured an 80-inch sleeper cab. Engine availability was from 180 to 335 horsepower. Buyers could choose from 20 optional transmissions ranging from 4 to 12 speeds. *Ron Adams collection*

The BC series was produced for three years, from 1959 to 1961. Brown Bros. Inc. of Curwensville, Pennsylvania, selected a sleeper cab for driver comfort on this BC-220. The trailer appears to be a Trailmobile. *Neil Sherff*

A newcomer to the family in 1962 is the new Loadstar series. This 1600 model was the lightweight tractor. The standard engine was the V-304. Optional engines were the V-266, the BG-265 gas engine, and two diesels—the D-301 and the D-354. A four-speed transmission was standard with the Select-O-Matic as an option. This 1600 is pulling a Fruehauf trailer. *International*

Here we have another 1600 model, this time in the form of a straight truck with a rack body. The specs for the straight truck were basically the same as the tractor shown on the previous page. There was a selection of 12 different gas and diesel engines available as options. *International*

This C-100 was in the pickup class. Although it was no big-time truck, it did haul big-time freight, so the sign says. Dick Meador of Dublin, Virginia, was the owner who leased it to Michael Preston Transportation Co., also of Dublin, Virginia. The standard engine was the V-266 with the BD-240 six or the V-304 V-8 as an option. *Theda's Studio*

This head-on shot shows a very nice view of what the R series looked like from the front. The model and whether it is a tandem or single axle is unknown. Also unknown is the gentleman's name. The trailer is a Fruehauf. Williams Transport Inc. of Cyril, Oklahoma, owns the rig. *W. E. Van Vacter*

Belger Cartage Service Inc. of Kansas City, Missouri, was mainly involved in heavy hauling. They also had several other types of equipment in the fleet. One of those trucks was this CO-200 with a refuse body. Standard engine was the RD-406 and it ran a five-speed transmission with overdrive. Belger selected the standard cast spoke wheels. Belger has been in business since 1919. *Warner Studio*

The slogan was "The blue-eyed Indians roam the Navajo trails." By 1962, the trucks for Navajo Freight Lines Inc. of Denver, Colorado, were roaming the Navajo trails from coast to coast after purchase of General Express Ways Inc. of Chicago, Illinois. Leading them across these trails was a huge fleet of DCO-405 Emeryvilles. Navajo was a big user of Internationals. This tractor is probably Cummins powered on a short, tight wheelbase. Navajo selected the 72-inch sleeper cab and the optional disc wheels. The trailer is a Fruehauf. *Robert Parrish*

The F-1800 series was the biggest in the Loadstar line. Twelve engines were offered for the Loadstar models with horsepower ranging from 113 to 197, including diesel and LPG. International T-35 five-speed transmissions were standard. T-34 and T-36 overdrives were available at no extra charge. The optional main transmission included the T-76 10-speed Roadranger. The GVW ranged from 18,200 to 46,000 pounds. *International*

Denver-Chicago Trucking Co. Inc. was based in Denver, Colorado. They always had a wide variety of equipment and Internationals, like this DCOF-405. Some Emeryvilles were used between their eastern terminals, although their authority stretched from coast to coast. According to the numbering system, no. 306 was used on a Los Angeles to Phoenix and Denver run. This tractor was powered by a NH-220 Cummins Diesel. *Denver-Chicago Trucking*

This side view shows the DF-400 set up to be in a truck/trailer combination. Two standard engines were offered — the Cummins NHE-195 and the 6V-71-218 Detroit Diesel. Optional horsepower from 4 to 16 speeds was available. The standard rear end for a tandem was 34,000 pounds. The tandem permits standard weights from 46,000 pounds GVW to 79,000 pounds. *International*

Uregas Services Inc. of Moberly, Missouri, owned this VF-220. This tractor ran on LPG and featured the V-549 engine. The customer chose the standard cast spoke wheels. The brand name of the trailer is unknown. *Ron Adams collection*

A few extras like dual stacks and air horns fancy up this DC-405. Optional disc wheels were selected along with the 80-inch sleeper cab. Lundgren, based in either Iowa or Nebraska, was the livestock hauler using a Wilson possum belly livestock trailer. *Ron Adams collection*

The Thompson-Hayward Chemical Co. in Llano, Texas, used this R-200 tandem tractor to pull their Lufkin grain trailer. Thompson-Hayward was a manufacturer of De-Pester agricultural chemicals. The standard engine was the RD-406 with the RD-450 and RD-501 as available options. Transmission was a five-speed overdrive with a six-speed automatic as an option. The standard wheels were the cast spoke type. *Lufkin Trailer Co.*

Here we have another DCO-405 as a truck/trailer setup. The unknown owner selected the 72-inch cab and optional disc wheels. The wheelbase was probably 212 inches. Optional engines were available from 190 to 335 horsepower. Transmission selection was from 4 to 12 speeds. The truck was leased to John Nix Transportation Inc. Notice the overdrive Roadmaster decal above the step. *Ron Adams collection*

Another addition to the line in 1963 was the new Fleetstar series that replaced the BC line. The standard engine was the NH-230 Cummins diesel with the 6-71N 238 horsepower as an option. Transmissions ranged from 5 to 16 speeds. The standard front end was 9,000-pounds capacity and the rear was 34,000-pounds capacity. This F-2000-D was picking up a new Heil gasoline tank trailer. The customer is unknown. *Heil Company*

In 1962, the line of the "stars" began with the Loadstar. Then, in 1963, the Fleetstar was introduced. We now add another "star" to the line and that begins the all-new CO-Loadstar. It was the baby of the cab over engine models. This CO-1800 featured the standard V-345 gas engine. The standard GVW was 24,000 pounds and the standard GCW was 40,000 pounds. The wheelbase ranged from 89 inches to 192 inches. Its purpose was mainly for city delivery work. The Strickland Transportation Co. Inc. of Dallas, Texas, used the CO-Loadstar in their network of terminals from San Antonio to Chicago and Boston. *Strickland Transportation Co.*

Here we see a variety of models. They are a DCO-405 Emeryville, an R series, and a B series. The DCO-405 is pulling a Trailmobile reefer trailer and the R is pulling a Brown reefer trailer. Notice on the Brown trailer that there is only one wheel well above the trailer tandem. The fleet is owned by Rockingham Poultry Co. of Broadway, Virginia. *Rockingham Inc.*

Here we have another International fleet shot. The fleet consists of two CO-Loadstars, a Metro series, a VCO, an AC series, and a DCO-405 Emeryville. There is also a Chevrolet pickup. Saunders Truck Rental Systems Inc. of Birmingham, Alabama, owns the fleet. The trailer is a Trailmobile. *Saunders Truck Rental*

Stokely Van Camp Inc. of Indianapolis, Indiana, owns this Fleetstar F-2000-D. It is seen here pulling a Fruehauf drop deck trailer. The load consists of an FMC green pea combine and an Oliver 1750 tractor. *Ron Adams collection*

This fleet of Loadstar 1800s is in the city delivery fleet of Ryder Truck Lines Inc. of Jacksonville, Florida. Notice the old round nose rib side trailers backed up at the dock. Also notice that one truck featured cast spoke wheels while the other featured disc wheels. *Ryder Truck Lines Inc.*

This D-405 was taking a break in a roadside rest area after a long, hard climb. This all-aluminum tractor was rated at 32,000 pounds GVW and 79,000 pounds GCW. Engine horsepower ranged from 210 to 335. Three Rolls-Royce engines were also available. The driver relaxed in the comfort of the air conditioning. Optional disc wheels were selected. Notice that this tractor had single headlights instead of dual headlights. The brands of the trailers and the undercover loads are unknown. *Brian Williams*

The DCOT-405 was equally as popular as the DCOF-405. The Transport Company of Fort Worth, Texas, owned this DCOT-405. It pulled an 8,000-gallon Trailmobile gasoline tank trailer. The names of the two gentlemen are unknown. *Bill Wood Photo Co.*

The D-400 series offered two hood sizes — the long and the short. This DCF-400 had the 92 BBC. The standard engine was the 6V-71N Detroit Diesel. The standard NH-180 was offered but not in this model. Optional engines were the V8-235 and the V8-265 Cummins, and the 260, 290, and 318 Detroit Diesels. Ruan Transport Corp. of Des Moines, Iowa, was the owner of the tractor and Fruehauf gasoline tanker trailer. Two sleeper cabs were available as options — a 110-inch and a 118-inch size. *Ruan Transport Corp.*

This CO-200 was busy hauling oxygen tanks on this Nabors trailer for the Gulf Oxygen Co. in Lake Charles, Louisiana. Standard cast spoke wheels were chosen all the way around. *A. J. Rybiski Jr. Photography*

This pair of V series tractors was LPG powered. The standard engine was the V-461 with the V-549 as an option. Standard cast spoke wheels were used all the way around. The Union Petroleum Corp. of Tulsa, Oklahoma, operated these two VF models. Brand names of the trailers are unknown. *Ron Adams collection*

The CO-Loadstar was popular in the straight truck line. The Carolina Container Company of High Point, Hickory, North Carolina, chose an all-steel 22-foot Black Diamond body (model FSC-22) to haul their manufactured corrugated boxes. *Black Diamond Trailers*

This DCO-405 tractor is shown pulling two twin bulk feed tank trailers. It featured the 54-inch cab and the optional disc wheels. *Ron Adams collection*

Moving household goods meant a lot of long distance or cross-country runs. This R-200 tractor was busy working for the Mayflower Transit Company of Indianapolis, Indiana, pulling a Trailmobile moving van trailer. A sleeper box was added as an option. *Harry Patterson*

This Fleetstar 2000 diesel was the right tractor for pulling this gasoline tank trailer of an unknown brand. It worked for the M.F.A. Oil Company of Columbia, Missouri. The standard engine was the NH-230 Cummins. Standard GVW was 43,000 pounds and the GCW was 79,000 pounds. The engine selections were Cummins and Detroit ranging from 218 to 270 horsepower. *Ron Adams collection*

Saunders Truck Rental System of Birmingham, Alabama, owned this VCOF-190. Saunders operated many rental stations with this tractor based in Houston, Texas. The standard GVW was 39,000 pounds with the GCW at 55,000 pounds. The standard engine was the V-401 with the V-478 as an available option. *Saunders Truck Rental System*

Here we have a DCF-400 with the optional 110-inch BBC sleeper cab. The standard engine was the 6V-71N Detroit Diesel with other engines available from 235 to 318 horsepower. A-A Midwest Rebuilders & Suppliers Inc. of Chicago, Illinois, owned this DCF-400 and pulled a Highway reefer trailer. *Brian Williams*

One of the bigger Loadstars was the 1850. This model featured the International DV-550 V-8 diesel that put out 180 horsepower. It used a five-speed transmission. The front axle had a 7,000-pound capacity and the rear axle had a 17,000-pound capacity. The optional engine was a DV-550 V-8 putting out 200 horsepower. Weickers Moving and Storage of Denver, Colorado, used their 1850 to pull this Fruehauf moving van. *Mr. Photo*

Oregon-Nevada-California (O.N.C.) Fast Freight of Palo Alto, California, ran almost all double trailers like this matching set of Trailmobiles. To pull the trailers, such as in this case, they used one of many DCO-405 tractors. It featured the 54-inch cab and optional disc wheels. *Brian Williams*

The CO series was the middle-sized cab over engine; bigger than the CO-Loadstar and smaller than the Emeryville. The CO-200 had the RD-406 engine as standard and a five-speed overdrive transmission. Transport-Trailer Inc. utilized these mobile containers that could be hauled on a flatbed trailer or on auto haul trailers to eliminate costly deadheading. *Ron Adams collection*

The driver of this VF-190 poses with his truck and shows off the long load for a photo shoot. Suwannee Transfer Inc. of Jacksonville, Florida, is the heavy hauler of this long concrete bridge span. The VF-190 had a GVW of 30,000 pounds and a GCW of 55,000 pounds as standard. The engine was the V-401 with the V-461 and V-549 available as options. *William Speer Photography*

Someone from International in Denver is handing a ring full of keys to someone from Navajo Freight Lines Inc. for the big order of new DCOF-405 Emeryvilles. These trucks have 80-inch cabs, optional disc wheels, air conditioners, dual air breathers, and dual stacks, which tells us that power might come from 318 horsepower Detroit Diesel engines. These tractors were used throughout Navajo's coast-to-coast freight system. *Le Donne's Studio Mr. Photo*

This Fleetstar F-2000-D is owned by Lufkin Trailer Co. in Lufkin, Texas. The purpose of this tractor is to deliver new trailers, such as these two dump trailers, to the customers and dealers. Lufkin chose the disc wheels option. *Lufkin Trailers*

Many of the big cities had their own fleets of many different makes and types of trucks. The city of Phoenix, Arizona, was no exception. This RDF-190 dump truck was diesel powered. The wheelbase varied depending on the kind of work the truck would perform. *Ron Adams collection*

Berman Sales and Leasing Co. of Pottstown, Pennsylvania, owned this DCO-405. It was on a lease agreement from Berman by Capitol Steel Structures Inc. of Baltimore, New York City, and Jersey City. The tractor is pulling an extendable Fruehauf flatbed trailer. This is what the standard DCO-405 looked like. *Shaner Studio Pottstown*

A new member to the family of cab over engines is the CO-4000. This new CO-4000-D was powered by the standard Cummins NHE-195 diesel engine. It featured a 50-inch aluminum cab, which was four inches shorter than the Emeryville cab. It had a 12,000-pound capacity front axle and a 23,000-pound capacity real axle. Optional horsepower ranged from 218 to 335 with either a Cummins or Detroit Diesel engine. This unit featured the optional disc wheels. The new member is pulling a set of Trailmobile doubles. *International*

Here we see four brand new COF-4000-D tractors on their way to being delivered. Three of them have the 83-inch cab and the last one has the 73-inch cab. The first one has optional disc wheels and the other three have standard cast spoke wheels. The standard engine on this model was also a Cummins NHE-195 diesel. Optional horsepower was from 218 to 335. Transmissions ranged from five speeds up to 16 speeds. These new CO-4000 models replaced the DOC-405 Emeryville. *Ron Adams collection*

Another new member to the line was the Payhauler 180. The GVW was 153,600 pounds and a 12V-71N Detroit Diesel engine powered it. Dual 18:00 x 25 inch 28-ply tires were placed all the way around. The capacity was rated at 45 tons or 38 cubic yards. *International*

This new Metro came onboard in November 1965. The M-1500s through the M-1700s did not use unitized bodies. The M-1500 had a 12-foot, 8-inch body. Little information is available on this model but in comparison, the M-1600 used the BG-241 engine and the M-1700 used the BG-2665 engine. *International*

Although the CO-4000 replaced the DCO-405 Emeryville, there were still some that were made in 1965. This one had the 80-inch cab and optional disc wheels. Beatty-England of Ottawa, Kansas owned this rig. Dual stacks meant that it was most likely powered by a Detroit Diesel. The trailer is an American. *Harry Patterson*

If you shopped at Sears you saved, and at the same time had the honor of having Sears deliver your goods with this Loadstar 1800. The body was a Unistel. The standard engine was the International V-345 gasoline V-8. The front axle was a 5,500-pound capacity with the rear being a 17,000-pound capacity. It featured a five-speed transmission. A six-speed Allison automatic was optional. Wheelbases ranged from 127 inches to 236 inches. This one featured the optional disc wheels. *Miller-Ertler Studios*

Here we have a pair of DCF-400s with the 92-inch BBC. Both of them belong to Indianhead Truck Lines Inc. of St. Paul, Minnesota. The truck in the foreground is pulling a Brown reefer trailer and the truck in the background is pulling a Butler tanker trailer. Indianhead had two divisions and used DCF-400s in both of them. *Chic Photos*

The driver of this CO-4000 sits proudly in the driver's seat as he and the truck and the five unidentified people pose for the photograph. Navajo Freight Lines Inc. of Denver, Colorado, was a big user of International trucks. Throughout the 1950s and the 1960s they continued to operate them. Navajo ventured into using the new COF-4000. This truck featured the 83-inch cab, an air conditioner for driver comfort, and optional disc wheels. It is seen here pulling a Fruehauf trailer commemorating Colorado science and technology. This photograph was taken in front of the Colorado State Capitol. *Navajo Freight Lines Inc.*

Here we see an R-190 for Mayflower Transit Co. of Indianapolis, Indiana. It featured the standard cast spoke wheels with an optional sleeper cab. Internationals, including this model, were very popular trucks in the moving industry. This R-190 is shown here pulling a Trailmobile moving van trailer. *Harry Patterson*

Curtis-Mathis manufactures all kinds of electronics for home entertainment. Their factories are located in Houston, Dallas, and Athens, Texas. Curtis-Mathis decided to use the CO series and Dorsey trailers to transport their products. *Photo Scope*

This Fleetstar F-2000-D was owned by Sterling-Emlenton and leased to Quaker State Products. It pulled a gasoline tank trailer. By the mid 1960s integral sleeper cabs were becoming a thing of the past. The Loadstar and Fleetstar series never featured sleeper cabs. An add-on box sleeper was available as an option. *Ron Adams collection*

Trans-Cold Express Inc. of Dallas, Texas, was a nationwide refrigerated carrier. One of the trucks in the owner/operator fleet was this DCO-405 Emeryville. It featured the standard cast spoke wheels, optional sun visor, dual air horns, an air conditioner for driver comfort, and the 80-inch sleeper cab. 1965 was the last year the DCO Emeryville was produced. The reefer trailer is a Fruehauf. *Neil Sherff*

Here we see a side view of one of the popular western setups, a truck/trailer combination. This DCF-400 with a 104 BBC has just been fitted with a new Clough tank body and Clough tank trailer. The standard engine was the International DVT-573 V-8 diesel with 240 horsepower. The optional engine was the Detroit Diesel 8V-71 available from 260 to 318 horsepower. The front axle was a 12,000-pound capacity and the rear was a standard 34,000-pound tandem drive. This DCF-400 featured the optional disc wheels. *Clough Equipment Co.*

This CO-4000-D played a roll in pulling a set of Kentucky moving van double trailers for North American Van Lines Inc. of Ft. Wayne, Indiana. This tractor featured the 83-inch sleeper cab and standard cast spoke wheels. The standard engine was the Cummins NHE-195 diesel. Cummins, Internationals, and Detroit Diesels were available as options with horsepower from 218 to 335. The standard transmission was a T-104 (5H-74) five speed. According to the spec sheet 30 different transmissions were available as options. *Brian Williams*

This Fleetstar 2000 was in the car hauling business, although it was empty at the time this photograph was taken. It was working for ARCO Auto Carriers Inc. of Chicago, Illinois. Troyler Inc. produced the trailer and tractor rack. Fleetstar models seemed to fit almost any kind of hauling. *Brian Williams*

This CO-Loadstar is another truck that is owned by the Saunder Truck Rental System of Birmingham, Alabama. This Loadstar was based at the Houston, Texas, branch. The standard engine for the 1600 and 1700 models was the V-304 gasoline. Diesel engines were optional. *Saunders Truck Rental*

Here we see a shipment of kitchen cabinets for Leisure World in Silver Springs, Missouri, and Cranberry, New Jersey. They were made by IXL Furniture Co. of Goshen, Indiana, and Elizabeth City, North Carolina. The products were being transported in this Fruehauf furniture trailer and being pulled by a CO-4000 International tractor with the 83-inch sleeper cab. *Ron Adams collection*

VCO production began in 1956 and the VCO was still being produced in 1966. Farley Fences Inc. of Bay City, Michigan, was delivering a load of fence posts with this VCOF-220. The standard engine was the International V-478 V-8 gasoline. The transmission was the T-402-5 speed. A total of seven optional transmissions were available including an MT series six-speed automatic. This VCOF-220 featured the optional sleeper cab. *Harry Patterson*

Armour and Company owned this CO-Loadstar. The body was made by Aero-Liner. The standard engine was the International V-345 V-8 gasoline. The spec sheet mentions nothing about LPG being available, but when you look at the fuel tank, it looks like it could be set up to run on LPG. *Aero-Liner Corp.*

The CO-4000-D that we see here is a short wheelbase tractor. Fairchild General Freight Inc. of Yakima, Washington, owns the rig. The short tractor hosts the 50-inch cab, has an air conditioner for driver comfort, and the optional disc wheels. The straddle carried trailer is used for hauling fruit from the orchards to the warehouse. The trailer holds 32 bins of apples, pears, etc. *Fairchild General Freight*

The Sunray DX Oil Co. of Kansas City, Missouri, chose this DCF-400 with the 104-inch BBC to pull this gasoline tank trailer. The standard engine was the International DVT-573 V-8 diesel with three Detroit Diesel engines as options. Notice that in 1966 International converted to the block letters. *Brian Williams*

ABC Truck Rental in San Antonio, Texas, chose this Loadstar 1600 as one of the trucks in their rental fleet. It was equipped with a Hobbs truck body. The standard engine was the International V-304 V-8 gasoline with a T-17 four-speed transmission. The fuel tank was an optional 31-gallon right-side mount. *Zintgraff Photographers*

The Georgia-Pacific Corp. of Tigard, Oregon, owned this COF-4000. The stretched out tractor was set up as a dromedary to carry extra freight on the "drom" body. This was common with many stretched out frames to make the most use of the available space. The wheelbases were 142-, 160-, and 190-inch options. The standard engine was the Cummins NHE-195 diesel. The optional engines were the International and the Detroit Diesel from 218 to 335 horsepower. Georgia-Pacific chose the 83-inch sleeper cab and the optional disc wheels. *Brian Williams*

Jones Truck Lines Inc. of Springdale, Arkansas, served 16 states in the Midwest area. Jones was always a big International user. Here we see one of their COF-4000 tractors pulling a set of American double trailers. This one featured the 73-inch cab and the standard cast spoke wheels. *Jones Truck Lines Inc.*

Navajo Freight Lines Inc. of Denver, Colorado, owned this Loadstar 1800 tractor. Navajo had many Internationals throughout their system. This one could have been based at Navajo's San Leandro, California, terminal. The standard engine for this model was International's V-345 V-8 gasoline. The wheelbases on this model ranged from 127 to 236 inches. *Bordanaro & Zarcone Photographers*

Olson Transportation Co. of Green Bay, Wisconsin, was also an International user. Here we have a COF-4000 with the 50-inch day cab. The standard engine was a Cummins NHE-195 diesel but a Detroit Diesel powers this one. The trailer is a Trailmobile. *Detroit Diesel*

This Fleetstar 2000 was owned by Tom Sayers Milk Transport of Lagrange, Ohio, and is pulling a 25-foot, 7-inch, 4,000-gallon Brenner milk tank trailer. The standard engine is the International RD-450 six gasoline. The transmission is the T-63 five-speed. Wheelbases were 132, 144, and 156 inches. *Brenner Tank Co.*

November of 1967 was the last month for production of the Fleetstar series. Matlack Inc. of Lansdown, Pennsylvania, had this F-2000-D pulling an LPG tank trailer. This tractor was powered by a Cummins NH-220 diesel engine. Matlack Inc. covered a large part of the eastern United States delivering almost everything that could be hauled in almost every different type of tank trailers. Fleetstars were produced from 1962 through 1967 when production ended. *Matlack Inc.*

As we say farewell to the old Fleetstar series, let us now welcome the new Fleetstar "A" series. This 2110-A model had a new style grille with the one-piece forward tilt fiberglass hood, and fenders. The standard engine was the International RD-450 gasoline six. The standard front axle had a 9,000-pound capacity and the rear axle had a 22,000-pound capacity. The standard transmission was the T-402 five-speed. Wheelbases ranged from 136 to 202 inches. This one featured optional disc wheels. *Ron Adams collection*

Once loaded, when hauling livestock, you had to keep moving in order to get the load to its destination on time without the loss of livestock. McCord Bros. Inc. of Frankton, Indiana, felt that this COF-2000 was the tractor to get the job done. It's seen here pulling a 40-foot Wilson possum belly livestock trailer. *Harry Patterson*

In the northwest, triple trailers were experimented with and did become a common sight on the northwest highways. Oak Harbor Freight Lines Inc. of Oak Harbor, Washington, was one of the companies that ran triples. They used a CO-4000-D tractor to pull the triple Brown trailers. Notice that the one trailer is for Peninsula Truck Lines Inc. This one joined the triple train through interlinking. *Oak Harbor Freight Lines*

This DCF-400 featured the 92-inch BBC cab. The standard engine was a Detroit Diesel 6V-71N of 218 horsepower. The front axle was a 12,000-pound capacity with the rear axle at 34,000-pounds capacity. Optional engines were Cummins up to 265 horsepower and Detroit Diesels up to 318 horsepower. The trailer is a Tri-axle Transport lowbed. *Barnard & Leas Mfg. Co.*

This F-210-D is in the form of a straight truck. The Standard Oil Co. used this one to deliver Chevron products in snow country. The standard engine for this model was the Cummins NH-180 diesel. The front axle has a 12,000-pound capacity while the rear came in at 38,000-pounds capacity as standard. Options were 16,000-pounds capacity at the front and 44,000-pounds capacity at the rear. This F series was used mainly for construction and oil field work. *Ron Adams collection*

Garrett Freight Lines Inc. of Pocatello, Idaho, covered the 11 western states and also North Dakota and Minnesota. Among the large fleet was this CO-4000 pulling a set of Comet and Fruehauf double trailers. The tractor had a 73-inch cab with an air conditioner and optional disc wheels. Notice that the second trailer is a wedge van. *Garrett Freight Lines Inc.*

Here we see a Loadstar 1600 at work with Ryder Truck Rentals. The 1600 had the International V-304 V-8 gasoline engine standard with an F-17 four-speed transmission. Front axle capacity was 4,700 pounds and rear capacity was 13,500 pounds. This one was based in Amarillo, Texas. *Ed Calton, Amarillo Daily News, Amarillo Globe Times, and Amarillo Sun News*

Chip Carriers Inc. of Omaha, Nebraska, that was a contract carrier, owned this CO-4000-D. The standard engine in this model was the NHE-195 Cummins diesel, however, with the dual stacks it could very well have been a 6V-71N Detroit Diesel. This tractor featured the 83-inch sleeper cab. The trailer is a Fruehauf furniture trailer. *Henry Kuehl*

This photograph commemorates 60 years of International history. This is what the Highwheeler auto buggy looked like. It was used as a passenger vehicle or a truck. Although it was big at the time, the giant unknown model behind it that featured the D series cab, dwarfs it. Try to fit those big balloon tires on the auto buggy! *International*

This F-250-D had a busy day hauling the huge storage tank somewhere in the western oil fields. W. M. "Billy" Walker Inc. of Hobbs, New Mexico, owned the truck. The bumper and grille guard combo were a must for this type of work. The standards on this model were the NH-200 Cummins diesel, with 16,000-pound front axle, and 50,000-pound rear axle. An 18,000-pound front axle and a 65,000-pound rear axle were available as options. A Cummins engine of up to 262 horsepower was the optional engine. This truck is featured on a 259-inch wheelbase. Mr. Walker chose the optional disc wheels. Notice the chrome radiator shell. *Ron Adams collection*

The year 1967 was the last for the CO-4000 series. This COF-4000-D was in a fleet at Superior Forwarding Co. of St. Louis, Missouri. It featured the 50-inch cab and standard cast spoke wheels. It is seen here pulling a shiny new Fruehauf trailer. The spare tire for the tractor is located on the frame. Note that Superior is the oldest direct daily carrier between St. Louis, Missouri, and Little Rock, Arkansas. *Superior Forwarding Co.*

This 1967 VF-220 is a restored piece. Jim Taylor of Millville, New Jersey, owns it. The standard engine was the International V-461 V-8 of 266 horsepower. The optional engine was the big V-549. Although this tractor had a sleeper cab the specs say that a sleeper cab was not available on the VF-220. *Dick Copello*

Here we see a fleet shot of three Loadstars and a "V" series. Super Propane Gas Co. owns these four trucks. The three bodies and the trailer are Mississippi brands. *Mississippi Tank Co.*

Coming into the lineup in 1968 is the new CO-4070-A Transtar. This CO-4070-A is owned by United States Ceramic Tile Co. of Campton, Ohio, and is shown here pulling a Strick trailer. The standard engine in this new Transtar was the International DVT-573 V-8 diesel. More powerful engines were available up to the Detroit Diesel 12V-71. The cab was raised five inches to accommodate the larger engines. The standard was a 12,000-pound capacity front axle and a 34,000-pound capacity rear axle. The cab sizes stayed the same as the old CO-4000. This one featured the 83-inch sleeper cab. *Ron Adams collection*

One of the companies that used the DF-400 was Eastern Express Inc. of Terre Haute, Indiana. The standard engine was the Cummins NHE-195 diesel. It had a 12,000-pound capacity front axle and a 34,000-pound capacity rear tandem. Other optional engines were Cummins from 218 to 335 horsepower. The only Detroit that was available was the 6V-71N. This tractor featured the 114 BBC. Eastern covered an area from Denver to the East Coast and up to Boston. This photograph was taken in Missouri. The trailer is a Fruehauf. *Brian Williams*

The D-400 became the Transtar 400 in 1968. This Transtar DF-400 featured the 114-inch BBC. The 114-inch BBC had seven optional engines, the 104-inch BBC had 10, and the 92-inch BBC had 17. Randy Trucking, location unknown, owned the truck. It had an air conditioner for driver comfort, an add-on sleeper box, and the new square turn signals. It also featured the optional disc wheels. *Brian Williams*

Brassfield Trucking of Tulare, California, owned this Transtar 4070-A. It is shown here pulling a set of Utility flatbed trailers. The load appears to be empty fruit crates. The standard engine was the International DVT-573-B V-8 diesel. The front axle was 12,000-pound capacity and the rear was 23,000-pound capacity. This tractor featured the 73-inch cab. Wheelbases ranged from 106 to 152 inches. This one featured an air conditioner and the optional disc wheels. *Brian Williams*

Here we have another Transtar 4070-A. This Transtar featured the 50-inch cab on a 106-inch wheelbase. The driver had air conditioning as he drove down the road pulling a set of Fruehauf double trailers loaded with Fritos corn chips for the Frito-Lay Company. *Brian Williams*

This photograph shows a seven-year span of Internationals beginning with a DCO-405 from the early 1960s, up to the CO-4000 and the Transtar 4070. Each uniform-clad driver stands proud with his truck. The Emeryville is hooked up to a Fruehauf trailer, while the other trailers are all Highways. Williams Products Inc. of Elkhart, Indiana, owns the trucks. *Ron Adams collection*

Pirkle Refrigerated Freight Lines Inc. of Madison, Wisconsin, was a refrigerated carrier that hauled nationwide. Their fleet consisted of owners/operators with various makes of tractors. This Transtar 4070 was one of the tractors in the fleet. It featured the 83-inch sleeper cab and air conditioning for driver comfort. The load was kept cold in this Utility reefer trailer. Gene Olson was the owner of the Pirkle Company. *Brian Williams*

Garrett Freight Lines Inc. of Pocatello, Idaho, used a lot of the big International tractors in their fleet. Garrett also used the smaller Internationals in their city fleet. This CO was teamed up with a Hewitt-Lucas body that was based in St. Paul, Minnesota. The engine in this model was the standard V-304. *Ron Adams collection*

Southern Pacific Truck Service Inc. was operated by the Pacific Motor Trucking Co. of Burlingame, California. Here we see a fleet of 18 tractors, each featuring dual stacks. These trucks are CO-4070-As. Detroit Diesel engines, which were optional engines, might have been the power sources. They all feature the 50-inch cab and are set up to pull double trailers. Southern Pacific chose the optional disc wheels. *Southern Pacific Truck Service*

Here we see a portion of the oil field working fleet for W. M. "Billy" Walker Inc. of Hobbs, New Mexico. The F-230-Ds were earning their keep, each one performing a different job. Oil field rigging was not an easy task and it required capable equipment that could handle the work. "Billy" Walker felt that these F-230-Ds were just the right trucks for the jobs. *Ron Adams collection*

Working together as partners is this 180 Payhauler and the Bucyrus-Erie shovel. The 50-ton capacity was moved by a Detroit Diesel 16V-71N putting out 560 horsepower. This was a 4x4 drive system with dual 18:00 x 25 balloon tires all the way around. *PA Commonwealth Photography Service*

Ligon Specialized Haulers Inc. of Madisonville, Kentucky, had the honors of delivering 57 Christmas trees to the White House to surround the 76-foot-high Christmas tree that was delivered from Glenn Falls, New York, to Washington, D.C., for the Pageant of Peace Week. A Transtar 4070-A with a Fruehauf converta-flat spread axle trailer got the job done. *Transport Topics*

Watkins Livestock Trucking Inc. of Kentucky had this Transtar 4070 hauling livestock in this Fruehauf livestock trailer. Dual stacks most likely meant that a Detroit Diesel powered it. This Transtar featured the 83-inch sleeper cab with optional disc wheels. *Harry Patterson*

This Fleetstar 2010-A was based in Texas. This one is set up to do lightweight oil field and construction work with John Deere bucket and backhoe work. The standard engine was the International RD-406 gas six. Optional engines were the RD-450 at 199 horsepower, the RD-501 at 214 horsepower, the VS-401 at 206 horsepower, the VS-478 at 234 horsepower, and the FTVS-549 at 285 horsepower. Standard transmissions were available, as was the MT six-speed automatic. *Ron Adams collection*

This COF-4070-A was one of three trucks that were produced for the B & B Packing Co. of Chicago, Illinois. This truck was used for city deliveries in Chicago. It featured an 18-foot refrigerated body, a 6-71N-65 238 horsepower Detroit Diesel, a 10-speed transmission, a 34,000-pound capacity rear axle, and carried a 28,000-pound payload. It featured the 50-inch cab on a 160-inch wheelbase. *Transport Topics*

Lucky Discount Supermarkets chose this CO-4070-A to pull this set of Trailmobile double trailers for making deliveries. It featured the 50-inch cab and the optional disc wheels. The standard engine was the International DVT-573 V-8 diesel. The standard transmission was the T-441 nine-speed. A total of 19 other transmissions were available as options. *Brian Williams*

Interlines-Blankenship Motor Express used this CO 1600 for doing local delivery work. The standard was the V-304 V-8 gasoline engine that put out 193 horsepower. It featured the optional disc wheels. The body is a Brown. *Brown Trailers*

The Champion Oil Co. in Rock Rapids, Iowa, chose this COF-4070-A to pull the Trailmobile gasoline tank trailer. The optional disc wheels were chosen, and it featured air conditioning, the 73-inch cab, chrome bumper, chrome breather bonnet, and 5-inch chrome stack that meant it had to be powered by either a Cummins NHCT-270 or a Cummins NTC-335 diesel engine. The standard transmission was the T-129 (RT-910) 10-speed Roadranger. A total of eight other transmissions were available from 6 to 16 speeds. *Ron Adams collection*

A new addition to the Transtar line was the Unistar. The Unistar was developed at the San Leandro plant. This new CO-7044-A was a 4x4 all-wheel drive. A Jifflox dolly was optional. With the Jifflox dolly it could handle 40-foot trailers, 27-foot doubles, 27-foot triples, or twin 40s. Standard power was a Cummins 335 or an 8V-71 Detroit Diesel. Available optional power was a 12V-71 Detroit Diesel. It featured a 121-inch wheelbase with a 73-inch cab. The specs say that the standard wheels were 20-inch cast spoke. The disc wheels are most likely optional. *International*

Here we have another CO-7044-A Unistar 4x4 with the cast spoke wheels. It is leased to International Transport Co. Inc. of Rochester, Minnesota. It is shown here pulling a set of flatbed doubles carrying four Ford bucket tractors. Notice the cut of the bumper. This did save a little weight but the reason for this was to prevent damage to tires in case of an accident. It featured the 73-inch sleeper cab. The engine is a Cummins NTC-300. Notice on the right side of the cab the letters "FWD" that indicated that it was a 4-wheel-drive 4x4. *Harry Patterson*

TRUCKS

AM General: Hummers, Mutts, Buses & Postal Jeeps ISBN 1-58388-135-2
Autocar Trucks 1899-1950 Photo Archive ISBN 1-58388-115-8
Autocar Trucks 1950-1987 Photo Archive ISBN 1-58388-072-0
Beverage Trucks 1910-1975 Photo Archive ISBN 1-882256-60-3
*Brockway Trucks 1948-1961 Photo Archive** ISBN 1-882256-55-7
Chevrolet El Camino Photo History Incl. GMC Sprint & Caballero ISBN 1-58388-044-5
Circus and Carnival Trucks 1923-2000 Photo Archive ISBN 1-58388-048-8
Dodge B-Series Trucks Restorer's & Collector's Reference Guide and History ISBN 1-58388-087-9
Dodge C-Series Trucks Restorer's & Collector's Reference Guide and History ISBN 1-58388-140-9
Dodge Pickups 1939-1978 Photo Album ISBN 1-882256-82-4
Dodge Power Wagons 1940-1980 Photo Archive ISBN 1-882256-89-1
Dodge Power Wagon Photo History ISBN 1-58388-019-4
Dodge Ram Trucks 1994-2001 Photo History ISBN 1-58388-051-8
Dodge Trucks 1929-1947 Photo Archive ISBN 1-882256-36-0
Dodge Trucks 1948-1960 Photo Archive ISBN 1-882256-37-9
Ford 4x4s 1935-1990 Photo History ISBN 1-58388-079-8
Ford Heavy-Duty Trucks 1948-1998 Photo History ISBN 1-58388-043-7
Ford Medium-Duty Trucks 1917-1998 Photo History ISBN 1-58388-162-X
Ford Ranchero 1957-1979 Photo History ISBN 1-58388-126-3
Freightliner Trucks 1937-1981 Photo Archive ISBN 1-58388-090-9
FWD Trucks 1910-1974 Photo Archive ISBN 1-58388-142-5
GMC Heavy-Duty Trucks 1927-1987 ISBN 1-58388-125-5
International Heavy Trucks of the 1950s: At Work ISBN 1-58388-160-3
International Heavy Trucks of the 1960s: At Work ISBN 1-58388-161-1
Jeep 1941-2000 Photo Archive ISBN 1-58388-021-6
Jeep Prototypes & Concept Vehicles Photo Archive ISBN 1-58388-033-X
Kenworth Trucks 1950-1979 At Work ISBN 1-58388-147-6
*Mack Model AB Photo Archive** ISBN 1-882256-18-2
*Mack AP Super-Duty Trucks 1926-1938 Photo Archive** ISBN 1-882256-54-9
*Mack Model B 1953-1966 Volume 2 Photo Archive** ISBN 1-882256-34-4
*Mack EB-EC-ED-EE-EF-EG-DE 1936-1951 Photo Archive** ISBN 1-882256-29-8
*Mack FC-FCSW-NW 1936-1947 Photo Archive** ISBN 1-882256-28-X
*Mack FG-FH-FJ-FK-FN-FP-FT-FW 1937-1950 Photo Archive** ISBN 1-882256-35-2
*Mack LF-LH-LJ-LM-LT 1940-1956 Photo Archive** ISBN 1-882256-38-7
*Mack Trucks Photo Gallery** ISBN 1-882256-88-3
New Car Carriers 1910-1998 Photo Album ISBN 1-882256-98-0
Peterbilt Trucks 1939-1979 At Work ISBN 1-58388-152-2
Refuse Trucks Photo Archive ISBN 1-58388-042-9
Studebaker Trucks 1927-1940 Photo Archive ISBN 1-882256-40-9
White Trucks 1900-1937 Photo Archive ISBN 1-882256-80-8

RAILWAYS

Burlington Zephyrs Photo Archive: America's Distinctive Trains ISBN 1-58388-124-7
Chicago & North Western Passenger Trains of the 400 Fleet Photo Archive ISBN 1-58388-159-X
Chicago, St. Paul, Minneapolis & Omaha Railway 1880-1940 Photo Archive ISBN 1-882256-67-0
Classic Streamliners Photo Archive: The Trains and the Designers ISBN 1-58388-144-x
Freight Trains of the Upper Mississippi River Photo Archive ISBN 1-58388-136-0
Great Northern Railway 1945-1970 Volume 2 Photo Archive ISBN 1-882256-79-4
Great Northern Railway Ore Docks of Lake Superior Photo Archive ISBN 1-58388-073-9
Illinois Central Railroad 1854-1960 Photo Archive ISBN 1-58388-063-1
Locomotives of the Upper Midwest Photo Archive: Diesel Power in the 1960s and 1970s ISBN 1-58388-113-1
Milwaukee Road 1850-1960 Photo Archive ISBN 1-882256-61-1
Milwaukee Road Depots 1856-1954 Photo Archive ISBN 1-58388-040-2
Show Trains of the 20th Century ISBN 1-58388-030-5
Soo Line 1975-1992 Photo Archive ISBN 1-882256-68-9
Steam Locomotives of the B&O Railroad Photo Archive ISBN 1-58388-095-X
Streamliners to the Twin Cities Photo Archive 400, Twin Zephyrs & Hiawatha Trains ISBN 1-58388-096-8
Trains of the Twin Ports Photo Archive, Duluth-Superior in the 1950s ISBN 1-58388-003-8
Trains of the Circus 1872-1956 ISBN 1-58388-024-0
Trains of the Upper Midwest Photo Archive Steam & Diesel in the 1950s & 1960s ISBN 1-58388-036-4

More Great Titles From Iconografix

All Iconografix books are available from direct mail specialty book dealers and bookstores worldwide, or can be ordered from the publisher. For book trade and distribution information or to add your name to our mailing list and receive a **FREE CATALOG** contact:

Iconografix, Inc.
PO Box 446, Dept BK
Hudson, WI, 54016

Telephone: (715) 381-9755,
(800) 289-3504 (USA),
Fax: (715) 381-9756
info@iconografixinc.com
www.iconografixinc.com

BUSES

Buses of ACF Photo Archive Including ACF-Brill And CCF-Brill ISBN 1-58388-101-8
Buses of Motor Coach Industries 1932-2000 Photo Archive ISBN 1-58388-039-9
City Transit Buses of the 20th Century Photo Gallery ISBN 1-58388-146-8
Fageol & Twin Coach Buses 1922-1956 Photo Archive ISBN 1-58388-075-5
Flxible Intercity Buses 1924-1970 Photo Archive ISBN 1-58388-108-5
Flxible Transit Buses 1953-1995 Photo Archive ISBN 1-58388-053-4
GM Intercity Coaches 1944-1980 Photo Archive ISBN 1-58388-099-2
Greyhound in Postcards: Buses, Depots and Posthouses ISBN 1-58388-130-1
Highway Buses of the 20th Century Photo Gallery ISBN 1-58388-121-2
*Mack® Buses 1900-1960 Photo Archive** ISBN 1-58388-020-8
New York City Transit Buses 1945-1975 Photo Archive ISBN 1-58388-149-2
Prevost Buses 1924-2002 Photo Archive ISBN 1-58388-083-6
Trailways Buses 1936-2001 Photo Archive ISBN 1-58388-029-1
Trolley Buses 1913-2001 Photo Archive ISBN 1-58388-057-7
Welcome Aboard the GM New Look Bus: An Enthusiast's Reference ISBN 1-58388-167-0
Yellow Coach Buses 1923-1943 Photo Archive ISBN 1-58388-054-2

EMERGENCY VEHICLES

100 Years of American LaFrance: An Illustrated History ISBN 1-58388-139-5
The American Ambulance 1900-2002: An Illustrated History ISBN 1-58388-081-X
American Fire Apparatus Co. 1922-1993 Photo Archive ISBN 1-58388-131-X
American Funeral Vehicles 1883-2003 Illustrated History ISBN 1-58388-104-2
American LaFrance 700 Series 1945-1952 Photo Archive ISBN 1-882256-90-5
American LaFrance 700 Series 1945-1952 Photo Archive Volume 2 ISBN 1-58388-025-9
American LaFrance 700 & 800 Series 1953-1958 Photo Archive ISBN 1-882256-91-3
American LaFrance 900 Series 1958-1964 Photo Archive ISBN 1-58388-002-X
Classic Seagrave 1935-1951 Photo Archive ISBN 1-58388-034-8
Crown Firecoach 1951-1985 Photo Archive ISBN 1-58388-047-X
Elevating Platforms: A Fire Apparatus Photo Gallery ISBN 1-58388-164-6
Encyclopedia of Canadian Fire Apparatus ISBN 1-58388-119-0
Fire Chief Cars 1900-1997 Photo Album ISBN 1-882256-87-5
Firefighting Tanker Trucks and Tenders: A Fire Apparatus Photo Gallery ISBN 1-58388-138-7
FWD Fire Trucks 1914-1963 Photo Archive ISBN 1-58388-156-5
Grumman Fire Apparatus 1976-1992 Photo Archive ISBN 1-58388-165-4
Hahn Fire Apparatus 1923-1990 Photo Archive ISBN 1-58388-077-1
Heavy Rescue Trucks 1931-2000 Photo Gallery ISBN 1-58388-045-3
Imperial Fire Apparatus 1969-1976 Photo Archive ISBN 1-58388-091-7
Industrial and Private Fire Apparatus 1925-2001 Photo Archive ISBN 1-58388-049-6
*Mack Model L Fire Trucks 1940-1954 Photo Archive** ISBN 1-882256-86-7
Mack Fire Trucks 1911-2005 Illustrated History ISBN 1-58388-157-3
Maxim Fire Apparatus 1914-1989 Photo Archive ISBN 1-58388-050-X
Maxim Fire Apparatus Photo History ISBN 1-58388-111-5
Navy & Marine Corps Fire Apparatus 1836 -2000 Photo Gallery ISBN 1-58388-031-3
Pierre Thibault Ltd. Fire Apparatus 1918-1990 Photo Archive ISBN 1-58388-074-7
Pirsch Fire Apparatus 1890-1991 Photo Archive ISBN 1-58388-082-8
Police Cars: Restoring, Collecting & Showing America's Finest Sedans ISBN 1-58388-046-1
Saulsbury Fire Rescue Apparatus 1956-2003 Photo Archive ISBN 1-58388-106-9
Seagrave 70th Anniversary Series Photo Archive ISBN 1-58388-001-1
Seagrave Fire Apparatus 1959-2004 Photo Archive ISBN 1-58388-132-8
TASC Fire Apparatus 1946-1985 Photo Archive ISBN 1-58388-065-8
Van Pelt Fire Apparatus 1925-1987 Photo Archive ISBN 1-58388-143-3
Volunteer & Rural Fire Apparatus Photo Gallery ISBN 1-58388-005-4
W.S. Darley & Co. Fire Apparatus 1908-2000 Photo Archive ISBN 1-58388-061-6
Wildland Fire Apparatus 1940-2001 Photo Gallery ISBN 1-58388-056-9
Young Fire Equipment 1932-1991 Photo Archive ISBN 1-58388-015-1

RECREATIONAL VEHICLES & OTHER

Commercial Ships on the Great Lakes Photo Gallery ISBN 1-58388-153-0
Phillips 66 1945-1954 Photo Archive ISBN 1-882256-42-5
RVs & Campers 1900-2000: An Illustrated History ISBN 1-58388-064-X
Ski-Doo Racing Sleds 1960-2003 Photo Archive ISBN 1-58388-105-0
The Collector's Guide to Ski-Doo Snowmobiles ISBN 1-58388-133-6